NATIONAL GEOGRAPHIC
School Publishing

T0058645

Figuras

Edward Lincoln

PICTURE CREDITS
Illustration by Marjory Gardner (14–15).
Cover, 2, 4 (above), 5 (center & right), 6 (all), 7 (all), 8 (below right), 9 (all), 10 (left), 11 (below left & above right), 12 (left), Photolibrary.com; 1, 4 (below), 5 (below), Lindsay Edwards Photography; 4 (center), Swerve/Alamy; 5 (above left), Zefa Images; 8 (left), 11 (above left), 12 (below right), 13 (above left, above right & below), Getty Images; 8 (above right), Photodisc.

Produced through the worldwide resources of the National Geographic Society, John M. Fahey, Jr., President and Chief Executive Officer; Gilbert M. Grosvenor, Chairman of the Board.

PREPARED BY NATIONAL GEOGRAPHIC SCHOOL PUBLISHING
Ericka Markman, Senior Vice President and President Children's Books and Education Publishing Group; Steve Mico, Senior Vice President and Publisher; Marianne Hiland, Editorial Director; Lynnette Brent, Executive Editor; Michael Murphy and Barbara Wood, Senior Editors; Bea Jackson, Design Director; David Dumo, Art Director; Margaret Sidlowsky, Illustrations Director; Matt Wascavage, Manager of Publishing Services; Sean Philpotts, Production Manager.

SPANISH LANGUAGE VERSION PREPARED BY NATIONAL GEOGRAPHIC SCHOOL PUBLISHING GROUP
Sheron Long, CEO; Sam Gesumaria, President; Fran Downey, Vice President and Publisher; Margaret Sidlosky, Director of Design and Illustrations; Paul Osborn, Senior Editor; Sean Philpotts, Project Manager; Lisa Pergolizzi, Production Manager.

MANUFACTURING AND QUALITY MANAGEMENT
Christopher A. Liedel, Chief Financial Officer; George Bounelis, Vice President; Clifton M. Brown III, Director.

BOOK DEVELOPMENT
Ibis for Kids Australia Pty Limited.

SPANISH LANGUAGE TRANSLATION
Tatiana Acosta/Guillermo Gutiérrez

SPANISH LANGUAGE BOOK DEVELOPMENT
Navta Associates, Inc.

Published by the National Geographic Society
Washington, D.C. 20036-4688

Copyright © 2008 National Geographic Society. All rights reserved.
Reproduction of the whole or any part of the contents without written permission from the publisher is prohibited. National Geographic, National Geographic School Publishing, National Geographic Windows on Literacy and the Yellow Border are registered trademarks of the National Geographic Society.

ISBN: 978-0-7362-3838-0

Printed in the United States of America

19 18 17 16 15

10 9 8 7 6 5 4

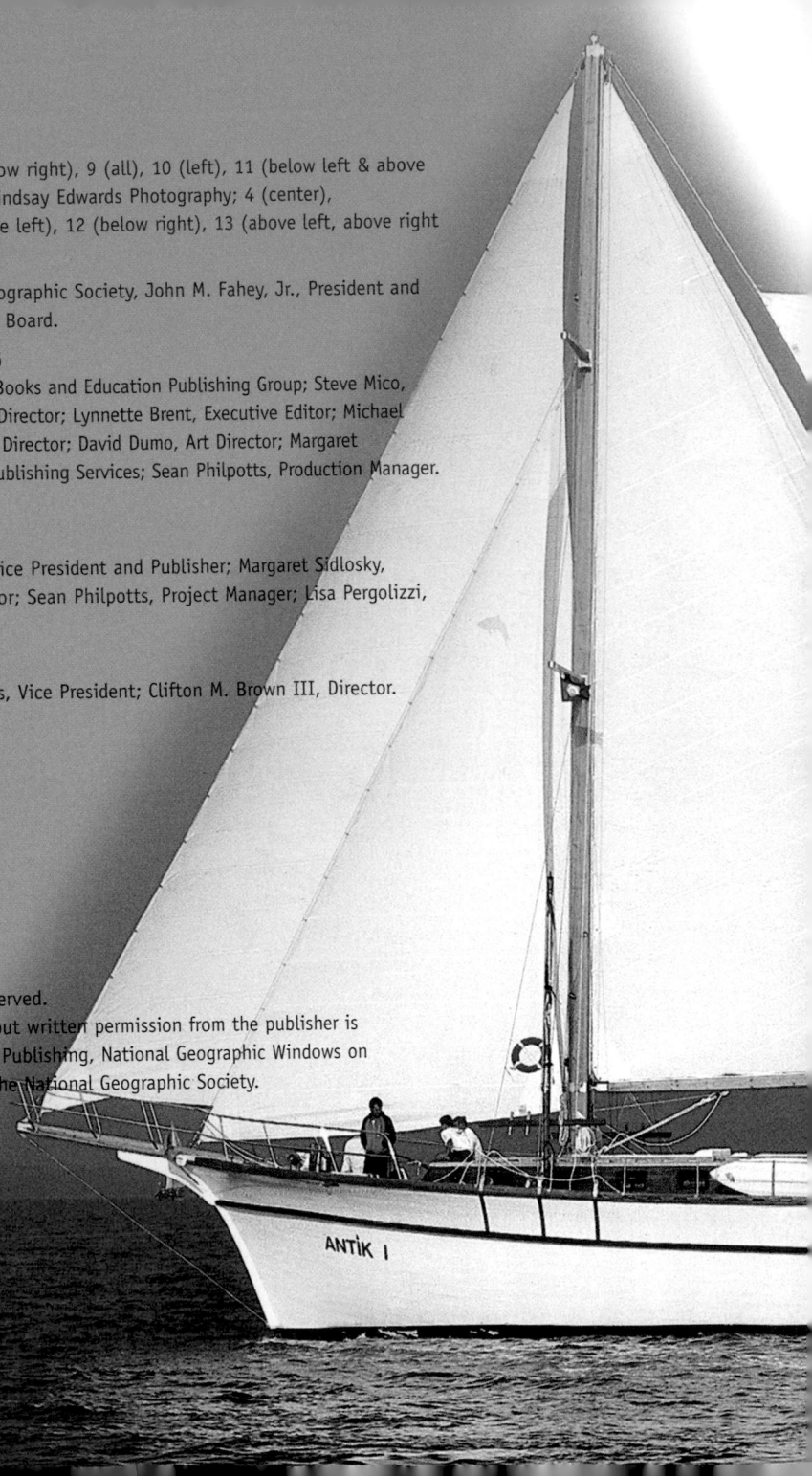

Contenido

Pensar y conversar	4
Círculos	6
Triángulos	8
Rectángulos	10
Cuadrados	12
Usar lo que aprendieron	14
Glosario ilustrado	16

Pensar y conversar

dianas

boleto

círculo

rectángulo

cuadrado

¿Qué figuras ven en estas fotografías?

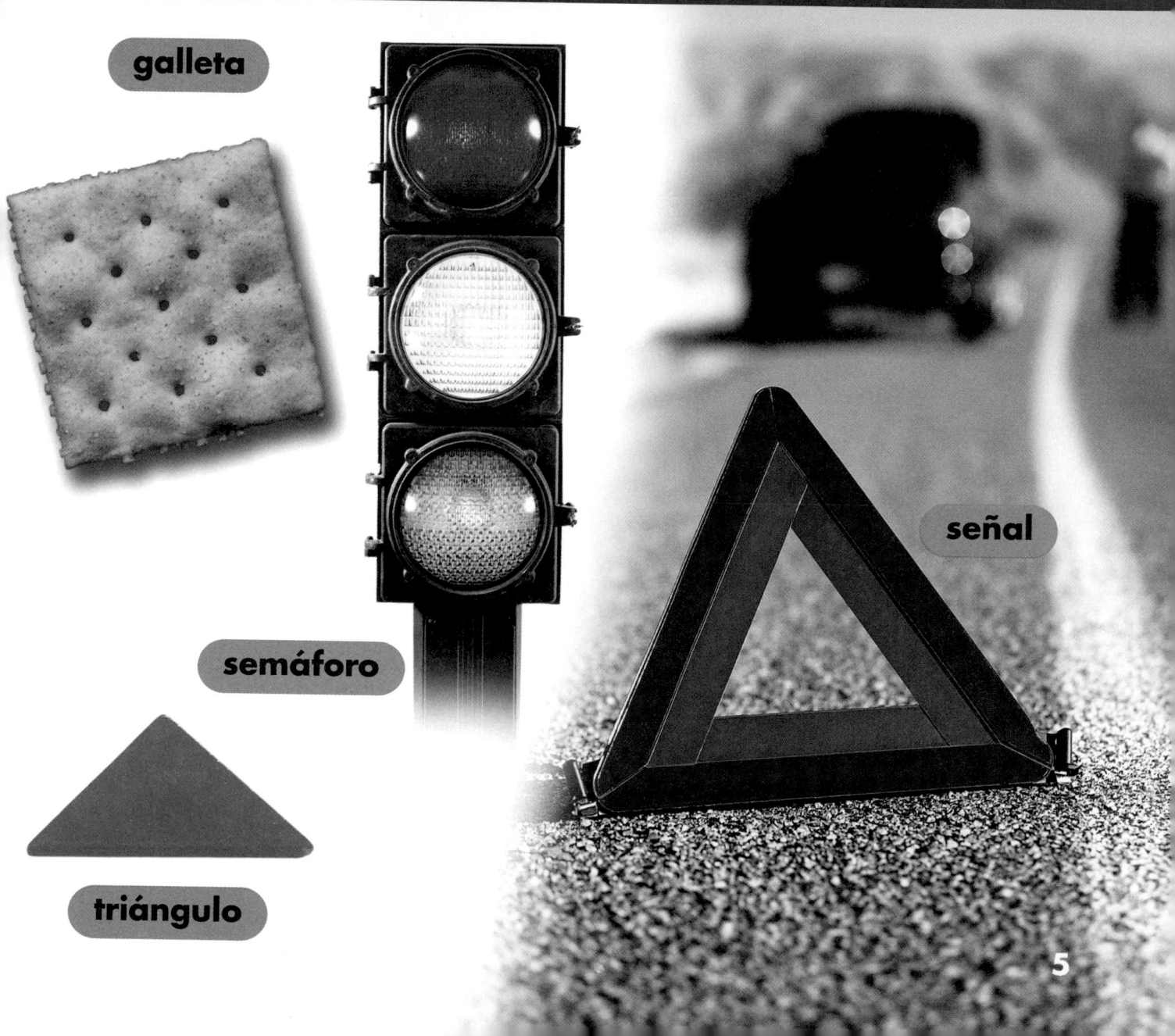

Círculos

Un círculo es una figura redonda.

12
1
2
3
4
5
6
7
8
9
10
11

Triángulos

Un triángulo tiene 3 lados rectos y 3 esquinas.

81
ANTIK I

Rectángulos

Un rectángulo tiene 4 lados rectos y 4 esquinas.

NATIONAL GEOGRAPHIC
Ventanas a la lectoescritura®
Matemáticas en Estudios Sociales
Banderas
Jan Pritchett

Cuadrados

Un cuadrado es un rectángulo especial. Sus 4 lados tienen el mismo largo.

WXY
9
#

Usar lo que aprendieron

En este dibujo, hay muchas figuras. ¿Pueden encontrarlas?

círculo

cuadrado

esquina

figura

lado

rectángulo

redonda

triángulo

Glosario ilustrado

círculo

rectángulo

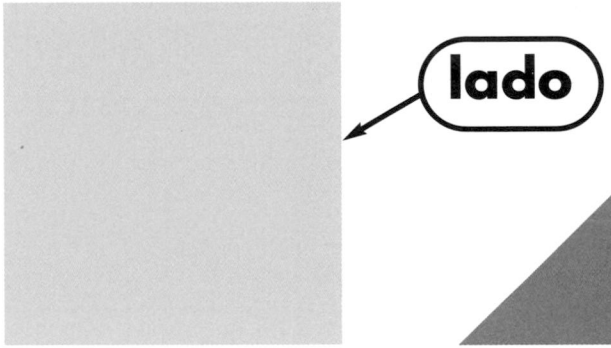

cuadrado

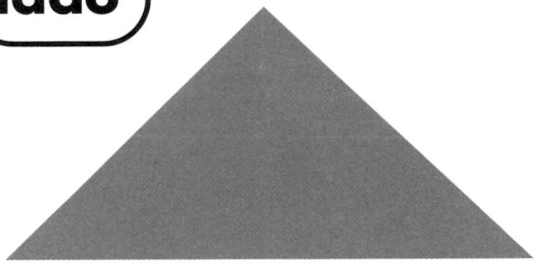

triángulo